Index: Page No.

Chapter 1:

TAROT HISTORY:

Tarot card was initially introduced as a card game in Italy in the early 14th century. It resembles with Egyptian images and symbols. Many changes took place as the Tarot reading progressed. Egyptian saints used Tarot to predict future. Every saint had different cards and its meanings. As the changes took place, hand painted cards were created. In the 20th century Tarot cards were machine printed.

Advert Waite reinvented Tarot cards in 20th century. He compiled all the cards and created an intuitive collection of Tarot cards. Pamela Colman Smith designed the cards, in the year 1910. Rider Waite Tarot Deck was invented and still continuing as standard Tarot Deck comprising of 78 cards. Later many more cards were created and are still in practice.

Chapter 2:

Why Tarot Cards should be used?

1) Tarot cards enables a perfect intuitive reading for seeking guidance, help and answers to a particular situation.

2) Like astrology or numerology, in Tarot we do not need any birth details. It gives answers to any situation or questions.

3) Tarot Reader needs to establish a personal connection with the cards. As you become one with the cards, it guides us and we become more and more intuitive every day.

4) The cards have various meanings; it guides us to give perfect answers in every situation or question.

Chapter 3:

Guidelines for using Tarot Cards:

1) The reader should be facing south and the person seeking answer will be facing north.
2) Tarot reading is done with specific purpose, question or seeking guidance.
3) The last card of Tarot deck represents the mindset of the person coming in. It will be the answer for his biggest question of life.
4) While doing Tarot reading always is peaceful, happy and composed. Never read Tarot cards when angry, upset or depressed.
5) If a card falls down while suffeling, do not use the card. It can be used later.
6) Never read Tarot Cards at negative places.
7) Never answer in low or depressed voice. Always inspire and motivate the client for solutions. Always radiate positive energy while doing tarot reading.

Chapter 4:

How to keep Tarot Cards energized?

1) Keep it in a wooden box.
2) Wrap it in silk or velvet cloth.
3) Light incense stick, light candle, keep crystals and offer flowers.
4) Use camphor (Kapur), flowers and shankh to energize the cards.
5) Charge the cards on full moon night or on day of eclipse. Do charge it once in a month.
6) Take a wooden bajot, place green cloth, spread rice, place the card of HIGH PRIESTESS (Tarot Devi), Idol of Ganesha, light diya and incense stick, offer flowers, bel leaves, tusli etc. Chant 5 time "Ganpati ath vasis".
7) Take 78 cards in hand and chant "Om Im Klim Chamundaye Viche".
8) For 22 major archana cards chant "Om Shivaya Namah" for 108 times.
9) For wands chants "Om Suryaye Namah" for 108 times.
10) For cups chant "Om gum ganpatye namah" 108 times.

11) For pentacles chant "Om him namah" 108 times.
12) For swords chant "Om Namo Narayanaye" 108 times.
13) Pray and command that: 1) I will use Tarot cards for benefit of others. 2) I will not harm anyone. 3) I will not use Tarot cards for any evil act or tantric work. 4) I will answer using my integrity. 5) I will give lot of respect to Tarot cards. 6) Tarot is dear to be and is my best friend. 7) I am sure that Tarot will guide me and always give me right answers.

Pray "HIGH PRISTESS give me success and fame in Tarot-Ameen"

Chapter 5

Description of and meaning of 78 Tarot Cards:

Total cards: 78

56 Minor cards and 22 Major cards.

56 Minor cards:

14 Wands   : 1-10 cards. Page, Knight, Queen & King.

14 Swords   : 1-10 cards. Page, Knight, Queen & King.

14 Pentacles   : 1-10 cards. Page, Knight, Queen & King.

14 Cups.   : 1-10 cards. Page, Knight, Queen & King.

Page, Knight, Queen and King: 16 Cards: Court cards.: Family, friends, neighbours, gives information about person's life.

1-10 cards: 40 cards. PIP cards, gives information about person's daily work and life.

Major Archana: 22 cards.: They can be seen as mind and spirituality of the person.

WANDS:

Element: Fire

Zodiac sign: Aries, Leo and Sagitarious.

Key points: Ambitions, creativity, energy, passion and spirituality.

Health issue: Blood pressure, body heat, acidity.

Business: Security guard.

Nature: Lot of travelling mentally and physically. Self made, success through time consuming act and hard work, sports personality.

CUPS:

Element: Water

Zodiac Sign: Cancer, Scorpion, Piecses.

Key points: Emotions, imaginations and intuitions, inner love, purity, easy life, wealthy life, affairs of the heart.

Health issues: Depression, skin irritations, cough, cold, blood related problems.

Business: Engineer, hospitals, schools, old age home, art, craft, dance,

Nature: Nature lovers, lack of time management, loves luxury life. Don't like interference of others, likes freedom, and operates less though mind and more with heart.

SWORDS:

Element: Air

Zodiac sign: Gemini, Libra and Aquarius.

Key words: Thinking, speaking, mental energies, a pure mind, energy of swards can be destructive but can also clear clutter.

Health issues: Gastric, constipation, nerves problems.

Business: Marketing person, sales man, counselling, businessman, lawyer, doctor.

Nature: quarrel type, always in tension, more expanses, gets hurt often, ambitious, practical, no emotions, and mental balance, calculative.

Pentacles:

Element: Earth.

Zodiac sign: Virgo, Capricorn and Taurus.

Key words: Body oriented, material world, health, money, work, security, solid reality.

Health issue: Diabetes, kidney problems, collastrol, heart problem.

Business: C.A., banking, jewellery, beauty parlour, designing, factory, decorative work, lawyer, share market, quick success, creativity, luxury, corruptions, money and material matters and powers.

Nature: Thinks, analyse and then decide. More patience, don't get angry easily, high morals and social values, loves disciplines, works as per set structure.

Zodiac Signs:

Aries	March 21 to April 20.
Taurus	April 21 to May 21.
Gemini	May 22 to June 21.
Cancer	June 22 to July 22.
Leo	July 23 to August 23.

Virgo	August 24 to September 23.
Libra	September 24 to October 23.
Scorpion	October 24 to November 22.
Sagittarius	November 23 to December 21.
Capricorn	December 22 to January 20.
Aquarius	January 21 to February 18.
Pieces	February 19 to March 20.

The Fool

Key words: Trust, opportunity, open mind, adventure.

Description and meaning:

The person is looking up in the sky. He doesn't know the way forward. The dog is cautioning him to be alert. There seems no way out as he is standing on the corner of the valley. He is holding a stick and food, sun in the background means that it's a bright sunny day. Time is favourable and he is happy. His cloths are fancy like an artist; he is holding a flower means he is very happy. He is very innocent and happy go lucky kind. Sun represents good luck. Be open minded, don't make preassumptions about your life. Be open to opportunities. Trust in universe to keep you safe then take leap into unknown. Should learn from past mistakes. He doesn't harm anyone; others are benefitted with his presence. Dogs represent loyalty and guardians. Helping nature.

Reverse: Close minded, assuming constraints, restlessness, impulsive, unfocussed, indiscipline, recklessness, not trustable, not innocent, over spending, no luck.

The Magician

Keywords: Consciousness, power, intentions, magic, success, masculine, yang, energy.

Description and meaning:

Magician has powers to control everyone. Red cloth means powerful energies. White cloth means that he is peaceful. Sign over his head means infinite, represents interaction of energy and matter. It represents wholeness of existence and it is inseperatable from life. Leaves mean growth. He is self reliant, self confident with strong will power. He doesn't like advice of other people. He will make preparations before starting new work, he will be prepared and will be successful. All round success, good times.

He is a good communicator, can convince everyone and is dynamic. He is knowledgeable. He will speak at the right time.

Reverse:

Misuses his powers. Black magician. No progress, unfocussed, unsupportive environment, lack of autonomy. Poor planning, not trustable, failure of project, weak, disempowered, unfocussed, selfish. Somebody may be using his energies. Something unethical or that will hurt anyone.

The High Priestess

Key words: Intuition, subconscious, secret, wisdom, yin, feminine, nature cycles, receptivity, inner wisdom.

Description and meaning:

2 pillars show stability. Security and protection. Spend time in solitude and silence, trust your intuitions. Practice meditation, hear your inner voice and tune in into your inner wisdom. Cross sign means union of male and female. Union with god. The vertical line is spiritual and male, horizontal line means infinite and harmonious. Time is not good for starting anything new.

Moon represents unconscious mind and feminine. It represents cycles of time, life and death. Has knowledge of past, present and

future. Universal knowledge and sudden gain.
Powerful 6th sense. Will take important position
in society.

Reverse:

Noise, lack of insight, gossip, the silent
treatment, frigidity, lack of integrity. Feminine
problems with monthly cycle, inability to look at
inner voice and intuitions. Reveals all secrets.
Chances of name being spoilt.

The Empress

Key words: Creation, abundance, cultivation, mother, sensuality, fertility.

Description and meaning:

The cloth represents creativity and time for fertility. Sign of Venus shows luxury, romance. Sitting on power chair means power to create. Object in the hand represents authority and power. Sitting like a queen means will play an important role in life. Strong attraction. Name, fame, money, sexuality etc. Will have good memory and intuition. Can start new work under name of female in the family.

Reverse:

Over abundance, too much of a good thing. Unwanted pregnancy, instability, emotional black mailer, miscarriage, no peace at home, mother issues.

The Emperor

Key words: Structure, leadership, foundation, endurance, authority, rules, order, father, no spirituality, materialistic attitude.

Description and meaning:

He is holding a power tool in his hand, which a symbol of power and authority. He is holding a yellow ball in his hand, which represents knowledge. He is aged, he is in a higher position in any family, society or organisation. He may also be a politician. He can handle any situation. He will have opportunity to carry on new things. He is dominating personality, imposing his ideas. He appears to be strong at the same time he is soft hearted. Good planner. He feels that he has to take care of everyone. He is a manipulative speaker.

Reverse:

Poor leadership. Abusing authority, misuses his position, ego driven, lack of structure. Unpredictable situation. Father issues. Rigidity. Money is stuck. Speaks bad words. Tries to prove himself right, even though he is wrong. Indicates complications in pregnancy for women.

The Hierophant

Key words:

Teaching, tradition, learning, belief, marriage, society.

Description and meaning:

It is a time to examine your beliefs. He is holding triple cross symbol in his hand. He is like an Egyptian guru.2 priests standing with him are those who believe in traditional religious values. It is time for knowledge, meditation etc. It is time to create positive vibration. The path will open if you follow knowledge and meditation. He is filled with mercy. He is knowledge and at the same time strict.

If this card arrears in reading for a marriage, they will prefer traditional way of marriage. He may be a yoga teacher, counsellor, government officer, union teacher etc. People come for taking his advice.

Reverse:

Rebellious, breaking free from tradition, bad conscious, unethical teacher, outdated beliefs. Divorce, splitting from spiritual growth. Doubty mind, not trustable, anyone can spoil his name.

The Lovers

Key words:

Union, bliss, partnership, choice, passion, sexuality.

Description and meaning:

There is an angel in the card who is giving blessings to the couple. Pure relationship is visible. Business partnership is possible. If done in name of female, it will be very successful. If this card appears in reading, you should get your work done by talking very sweetly. Possibility of new friend circle. Couple should focus on each other for fulfilment. The male partner may be seeking fulfilment, but the female partner is spiritual and already fulfilled, so there could be differences between them. Sun represents ambition, growth. Mountain indicates pilgrimage and spiritual path.

Reverse:

Interpersonal trouble. No chemistry between two. Lust and not love. Communication breakdown. Imbalance in relationship. Co-dependence on each other. Troublesome relationship triangle. Bad choices. Unrequired love. Unhappy lovers. Failure in relationship.

The Chariot

Key words:

Will power. Warrior. Determinations. Progress. Perseverance.

Description and meaning:

He is looking like a warrior; he is prepared for travelling for business. His chariot has sign of discipline. He is too disciplined person. The castle in back shows that they are influenced by old religious values. They are under influence of evil person or monster; they need to really come out of their shell to grow. He is not alone, there is someone with him. He is prepared when he is going. He holds a stick which represents power. He is wearing a symbol of his kingdom that shows power. He is ambitious. Good planner. May expect new vehicle. Good time to buy new house. Two colour lions show that he has to encounter positive and negative where ever he goes.

Reverse:

Delay in work. Fear holds you back. Scattered energies. Lack of focus. Travelling trouble. Cursing ahead. Going now here. Not confident. Egoistic nature. Stored emotions will flow out like a volcano.

Strength

Keywords:

Passion, inspiration, birth, opportunity.

Description and meaning:

Lions are associated with kings, royalty, strength and majesty. Mountain means there are some problems in life. Infinity symbol on head represents interactions of energies and matter. She is wearing white cloths and opening mouth of lion, so you should work in harmony of body, mind and soul. Have courage and passion while doing your task. Release fear and you will succeed. Women's help will enable success. With full conviction you can succeed. Flower ring on the top shows that lion is already in control. Means that you are in control of situation. They are merciful and sexual.

Reverse:

Weakness, out of control. Power imbalance, domination, submition, stubborn. Disconnection between ideal self and actual self. Problem in heart and blood. Egoistic.

The Hermit

Keywords:

Solitude, wisdom, guidance, introspection, withdrawal.

Description and meaning:

The lamp associated with light is a symbol of wisdom and knowing. Lamp gives us clarity. Knowledge is already there. Staffs are sign of power and magician. There is struggle in present day life. He looks stressed with issues and he would like to withdraw himself from everything. The white path is visible, he should go to a calm place and meditate. He will not share his things with anyone, so he will be more unhappy. Time is not favourable for relations. He is spiritual and religious. Can expect ex-lover but to accept or not is your choice. He is a good advisor and always gives right advices. He will have to stay with all.

Reverse:

Need for solitude. Social burn out. Private thoughts. Anti social. Not trustable. He gives wrong advice so nobody goes to him.

The Wheel of Fortune

Key words:

Movement, change, expansion, opportunity, destiny, luck.

Description and meaning:

Wheel means fortune and Egyptian symbol on wheel means that you should take knowledge from everywhere. Cloud and birds mean that at the moment there are problems but it will be all fine soon. Practice yoga, exercise and meditation for maintaining health. Don't stress yourself. When destiny favours, this card appears. There will be ups and downs, grab opportunity whenever it appears. If this card appears in outcome fortune will change soon. If it appears in lower cards, there is waiting time for fortune to change.

Reverse:

Stagnant, delayed, unwise investment, unlucky, slowdown, reconsider.

Justice

Keywords:

Ethics, logic, equilibrium, honesty, karma.

Description and meaning:

Very practical. As they are too practice, relationship suffers. Scale represents balance and equilibrium in giving and receiving. Pillars hold everything. If this card arrears in match making, it indicates that marriage alliance is possible. It is necessary to have balance in health. If this card appears in outcome of legal matter, it will be in our favour. If its card appears in surround, help will be available. If ant negative card appears along with this card then it will not be in our favour.

Reverse:

If there are problems in relations, court case is possible. There is no chance of justice. Everything is illegal. Fear of doing wrong. Derive wrong meaning of everything.

The Hanged Man

Keywords: Selflessness, stillness, sacrifice, devotion, surrender, new perspective, initiation.

Description and meaning:

The hanged man shown in the card is radiating patience, contemplation and surrender. He does not look in sorrow. Radiant glow is seen around his head. He is very genius, intelligent and clever. He is showing that greatest things will happen when you let go. Don't try to control every situation, make peace with uncertainty.

Something uncertain might happen when this card appears. It indicates disease or stuck issues. He has learnt from life situations; he may not be very successful. He forgives everyone but finds hard to get out of certain situations. Look at the situation from different perspective. You may need to sacrifice in order to move forward.

The sun in the card indicates beginning of spirituality. It is time to relax and hold back your energies for time.

Reverse:

It reflects ego in relationships, time to let go. Addiction is a possibility. Shows social pressure. If this card appears in love and relationship you must let go. Do not operate with sentiments rather give proper logical response to the situation. You may be hypocrite doing one thing and saying one thing. Be aware of the people who shows holier attitude and do not have this attitude yourself. You are wanting to lead a more spiritual life but you do not know how to do it. Do not over think over a situation.

Death

Key words:

Ending, transformation, closure of a situation, purging or regeneration.

Description and meaning:

The man travelling on white horse has cruel smile on his face. He is wearing cloths like a devil. There is a queen and a child in front of the horse. There is a man lying under the horse. He is holding a black flag on this left hand. As the name suggests this card does not mean death. One should forget the past events. It indicates end of a cause, relation or suffering. Prayers will work. Major crime may happen. It shows ending of something, it shows lust, destruction. It also shows end of a cycle. The soul leaves behind everything and walks on its life path. When one cycle ends the new cycle begins. It indicates birth of a child or new beginning. End of bad times.

It is time to get rid of what is no longer useful. Seek closure before new beginning. This may not be an easy change but it is necessary for the wellbeing. If you feel stuck it is time to let go. Free yourself from stagnant energies. Let go and trust in the universe, a new chapter is about to begin.

Reverse:

When this card appears in reverse it indicates lack of closure, repeating patterns, more to learn, attachment, running away and burning issues.

There is a delay in reaching a conclusion to some aspect of life. It is not time to move on, there is still ore to learn. If death card appears in reverse you are trying to escape some uncomfortable situations. Do not run away rather face and resolve the situation otherwise it will keep repeating in some or the other form. The person is tired mentally and physically. He seeks change but not happening.

For female it shows menopause issues. End of a friendship. Every hope will turn into disaster. Create enthusiasm to move forward in life.

Temperance

Key words:

Balance, integration, harmony, adjustment, healing and moderation.

Description and meaning:

In this card an angel is wearing a white robe and standing on clean water. Shows 2 wings and glow behind the head. Holding 2 cups in each hand. Transfers nectar from one cup to another. The sun is rising in the background. There is a triangle symbol on chest and a circle on the head.

This card means that the person can balance 2 aspects at one time like home and office. The person is serious, matchure and in discipline. There is grace of god. He is constantly thinking, having high will power so desires will be fulfilled. Does not reveal his thoughts to others, so might suffer. Take care of everything and lives in harmony with all. May indicate kidney problems.

Temperance is the card of integration and finding balance. Now is the time for adjustments. One or more things are coming up together to create something new. Change one thing at a time, see the result then change more things. Find balance before moving on, compromise may be necessary.

Reverse:

When this card appears in reverse it means out of balance, overemotional, not compromising, drastic change.

If experiencing disease, the trouble may increase. Power may reduce. There is difference between talks and actions. Many times, act like a child with erratic behaviour. Experiencing mood swings. In reverse this card indicates lack of balance. You may be over emphasising your feelings and ignoring your behaviour. In relationships you may be refusing to adjust or let go. May be compromising too much to please others. You try to make many changes at once. Make changes gradually and gently. You may be keeping important aspects of life separately from others. Integrate various aspects of life to feel more complete.

The Devil

Key words:

Indulgence, attachment, materialism, addiction, pleasure, lust, shadow, temptation, self-destruction, self-limiting behaviour.

Description and meaning:

The card shows devil with cunning smile. He is holding fire on left hand. Naked male and female standing helplessly.

Devil is a card of lust, indulgence and material pleasure. When the devil appears it shows darkness, negativity, jealousy, misuse of power, black magic, fear etc. Devil means the inner devilish nature of the person. In business it shows lust for money. In some way you are deceiving yourself.

When devil appears the person is negative, operates with high ego. The person has bad habits, bad behaviour. Self sabotaging behaviour. When appears for a pregnant lady, it might indicate miscarriage.

Reverse:

Breakthrough, taking control, breaking free, born again, rock bottom, enough is enough.

The Tower

Key words:

Chaos, sudden change, shock, distress, outburst, shaking things up, natural disaster, disruption.

Description and meaning:

Shows the explosion of tower. Two men are thrown out due to explosion. There is out burst of fire in dark background.

It means that suddenly something will happen and there will be hardly any time to control the matter. The tower is a card of shock and chaos. The system and structure of life is shaken up. The person should be sensitive to changes.

When this card appears it shows sudden expenses, sudden loss, unwanted pregnancy, poverty, sadness, lack, punishment, weakness, anxiety, rigidness, humiliation etc. Someone could have an emotional outburst. Natural disaster, relationship breaking, electric shock, bad news may be experienced. One should let go of old belief patterns. Drastic changes are required in your life.

Reverse:

Some emergencies, tension, mounting stress, release, averting disaster, shake it up. Making changes to avert disaster. Throw away clutter.

The Star

Key words:

Optimism, hope, renewal, cleansing, astrology, peace, connection, recognition.

Description and meaning:

A naked lady has pot in both hands, pouring water from both. She is trying to balance. Pleasant atmosphere in background, 8-point star is visible surrounded by many stars. It is a symbol of trust, should have faith. It indicates that hard time is over. Confidence will be built. Progress in study. Will be helpful to others, can expect better results. Name, fame and money will be received. It represents youth and beauty. The person is lucky, will be benefitted by water. Good news is expected.

The star brings optimism with new start. When this card appears trust in universe. You are on a healing path. Do what is practically required, look at spiritual and physical aspects of life. Be calm and still to heal completely. The star is a sign of success.

Reverse:

Hope without action. Unethical healer, inner doubt, show off. Tension, lack of inspiration, loneliness, positive turning negative. Lack of confidence.

The Moon

Key words:

Unknown, hidden things, unconscious, illusion, fear, confusion, deep emotions, doubt, indecision.

Description and meaning:

In this card sun and moon are seen into each other. Face of moon looks in stress. In water there is scorpion. Dog and fox are looking fearful.

When this card appears, it is a sign of warning. The person is living in illusion and material lust. He is emotional and confused. The person is unable to understand the situation. May get bad dreams. Will fear animals. Will be emotionally upset and in depression. Suddenly become low from high state. Moon represents mind, water represents caution and pillar shows strength.

Moon is the card of darkness, illusion and the unconscious. You may be hiding something from self and others. You are feeling confusion and fear. Moon advices to understand things before taking action. This card also represents natural cycles, menstruation, or the season change.

Reverse:

Self-deception, self-doubt, being lost, avoiding risk, only seeing what you want to see. Unresolved questions, black magic or negative energy may be present.

The Sun

Key words:

Clarity, inspiration, enlightenment, vitality, positivity, affirmation, happiness, success.

Description and meaning:

Sun is bright and pleasant. The horse is peaceful, sunflowers blossoming in back ground. The child looks very happy and holding a red flag in hand.

When this card appears in the reading you can expect good news. Name, fame and money is for sure. Will get results for actions, success on the cards. Positive attitude, active and energetic approach. Joy, friendship, victory, optimism, desire fulfilment. Freedom from bad times. The child is expressing victory which shows that you will receive all your rights. Indicates good health and travel. Happy moments are experienced.

The sun is a card of light. When this card appears, you will have greater clarity and understanding. It is time to share your accomplishments and share them with all. Don't be afraid to shine. Let your inner child shine. Be playful, creative and curious. If it appears in outcome card it means "yes".

Reverse:

Feeling dim, burnout, can't let loose, sunburn, self centred, show off, competition, low power and low strength, struggle.

Judgement

Key words:

Judgment, rebirth, review, objectivity, awakening, signs, true calling.

Description and meaning:

An angel in the card is spreading wings and blowing a trump. He is having a cross. Dead bodies are standing out of grave and spreading arms.

Judgement is a card of drastic change. It shows 2nd chance. If it appears for exam, may have to appear twice to clear it. The current phase of life is coming to an end. Now it is a time to look for what comes first. If this card appears for marriage, may divorce but will remarry again. It is seeking justice from god, let go of orthodox nature.

Change is unavoidable if this card appears in a reading. Grab new opportunity. End of bad relationships. Be honest with yourself. You may expect greater benefits. Pay attention to your ideas, all dreams are possible.

Reverse:

Judgemental, confused about your path, too much noise, not trusting your intuition, fear of death, guilt, stress.

The World

Key words:

Integration, completion, fulfilment, holistic, victory, culmination, synthesis, the earth, voyage.

Description and meaning:

The card shows oval garland of flowers, in the centre of it there is a lady. She is wearing a silk cloth. She is dancing and holding sticks in both hands. In the four corners there is face of a lady, eagle, lion and ox.

The world card indicates both ending and new beginning. You have learnt lesions from past and it is time to move on. Fulfilment, your work will get done. The person will be very balanced will execute task very well. This card means victory, name, fame and money.

It says that moves beyond your personal quest and have bigger thoughts for earth.

Reverse:

Incomplete, disappointment, repetition, private victory, clinging to the past, stuck.

Ace of Cups

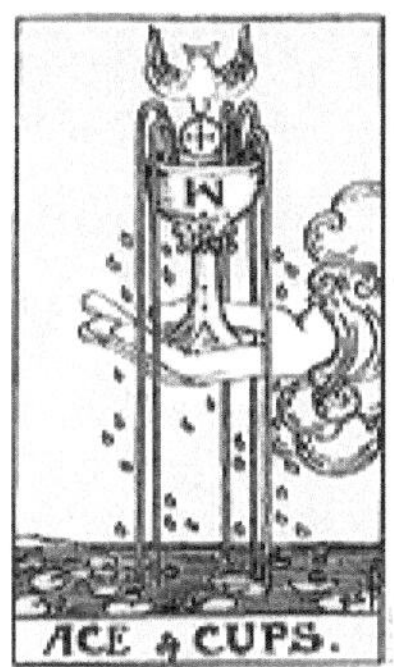

Key words:

Joy, new love, spiritual awakening, opening to emotion, gift from the heart, love letter, personal connection, introspective insight, wakening intuition.

Description and meaning:

In this card water is flowing through the cup from 5 points. It is surrounded by clouds. Lotus is blossoming. Bird and + sign are visible. When this card appears look for new opportunities of love, friendship or spiritual growth.

It indicates positive thinking, trustworthiness, creative projects etc. This is an opportunity for intimacy and pleasure. The person for whom this card appears is loveable, happy, helpful. This indicates a fresh start emotionally. The ace of cups indicates conception, a pregnancy, or a birth.

It also indicates opening of intuition – a chance to tune in into your higher self. When this card appears be ready to subtle changes and pay attention to your dreams.

Reverse:

Denial, ignoring intuition, emotional disconnect, hiding feelings, giving up something pleasurable. This is not right time. Untrustworthy, betrayal.

Two of Cups

Key words:

Union, love, support, trust, equality, attraction, cooperation, compromise.

Description and meaning:

In this card a male and female is exchanging cups. Two of cups is a card of union – two or more things coming together to create something new. Both are lovers, caring and sharing with each other. Energy meeting is showing as a union and a lion type face is witnessing the union. It means proposed partnership, proposal, love and pure energy made for each other. If any court matter is there it will be resolved with mature understanding.

This card represents romantic attraction, a marriage, coming to a compromise. Mutual support in a relationship. Friendship, equality between two people or more groups of peoples. It represents emotional support and equality.

Reverse:

Disharmony in relationships, arguments, break-up, refusing emotional connection, taking space apart, power imbalance, unrequited love, bad date. Misunderstanding, ego problem, separation or divorce.

Three of Cups

Key words:

Friendship, celebration, entertainment, fun, success, ritual, dancing.

Description and meaning:

In this card three women are holding cups, enjoying and celebrating. When this card appears, it is time to rejoice in the friendship. This card means that you have friends who truly care and support you.

It indicates that a new relationship will grow into a real friendship. It indicates wedding in the family, birthday celebration, birth of a new child, reunion, business success, progress in study, recovery from disease etc.

In romantic relationship when this card appears it means mutual attraction and affection. It means positive growth from the emotional union of two or more people.

Reverse:

Trouble with friends, loneliness, no friends, left out, antisocial, jealousy in friendship, gossip, excessive partying, unhealthy friendship. Failure in love, misunderstanding, triangle love story.

Four of Cups

Key words:

Withdrawal, contemplation, dissatisfaction, boredom, daydream, incubation.

Description and meaning:

In this card a sad person is sitting below the tree. This card indicates withdrawal from an emotional situation. He is receiving a fourth cup from the sky, but he is not looking at it and is unhappy within himself. He cannot grasp the opportunities he is having. He is tired of a situation and lacking the emotional resources to proceed.

It is time to look within and find inspiration from within. Four of cups may be advising you to withdraw for a time being, not to get stuck and move on after taking rest. Use the time to seek inspiration so soon you can continue forward.

Reverse:

Burnout, pushing through, ignoring emotions, extended vacation, disengagement.

Five of Cups

Key words:

Loss, grief, disappointment, regret, fear, guilt, pessimism, turning point.

Description and meaning:

In this card a person is standing in black robe with his head down. In his front there are 3 fallen cups. Two cups are up straight in back side. The five of cups represents loss. The person is sad, ready to leave everything and run away.

When this card appears feeling of disappointment, regret, sadness and grief are at work. The loss suffered is something dear to the heart. The lesion to be learnt from this card is that with loss also comes change and opportunity. Two cups in the background indicates that still there is support and opportunity available. It indicates to look at new positive side of the matter.

Reverse:

Wallowing in sorrow, clinging to the past, time to move on, worst is over.

Six of Cups

Keywords:

Kindness, nostalgia, the past memories, care, protection, childhood, childish.

Description and meaning:

In this card two ladies are taking to each other. One is a teenager and other is a grownup lady. All the cups are filled with flowers. In the background a soldier is going.

The six of cups is a card of friendship, innocence and childhood. When this card appears in a reading be thankful for small gestures of kindness and find ways that can brighten the day of another.

If you have difficulty in your life turn into your inner child and past. That gentle innocent and wise part of yourself that has always been with you for guidance. There is no situation of any lack, everything is available. Will get help from senior person. Something of the past will be useful to you now. The six of cups represents arrival of new person, beautifying your home or choosing a gift. Simplicity and authenticity are key.

Reverse:

Selective memory, painful memories, immaturity, regression.

Seven of Cups

Key words:

Fantasies, many choices, visualizing, altered states, creative brain storming, too good to be true.

Description and meaning:

The shadow of the man is looking into the sky, seven cups are filled with different things. Only one hand of the man is visible, he looks confused.

The seven of cups is a card of choices and fantasies the man is frightened, he is scattered. It means that you have many choices available to you that indecision will prevent you from choosing anything. Nothing is clear in the mind, fantasies and day dreaming. Not certain of what to do next.

This card could indicate the need to shake things up in order to recognise alternative path you could take. The seven of cups also indicates altered state of consciousness, dreaming and visualization. Beware of taking decisions after analyzing everything.

Reverse:

Lack of imagination, pragmatic actions, losing touch with reality, substance abuse, escapism.

Eight of Cups

Key words:

Leaving behind, moving on, retreat, emotional restoration, call of spirit, travel, abandonment.

Description and meaning:

It is new moon night, sun and moon are visible together. Moon represents mind and sun represents soul. There are eight cups but the man is depressed in going in other direction. There are mountains at a distance, he is leaving home going away. It indicates that he has no interest or someone have left him.

When this card appears in a reading for marriage, it is not favourable. This is the card of letting go and moving on. It shows pain, is seeking emotions. It could literally mean leaving – changing homes, ending a relationship, quitting a job, going on a trip to find yourself, leaving behind hopes and dreams.

When this card appears, you are tired of feeling disappointed and hopeless and ready to look for better things. This card indicates a craving for spiritual deepening.

Reverse:

Clinging, emotionally possessive, fearful of letting go, trying too hard, emotional reunion, feeling of emptiness.

Nine of Cups

Key words:

Emotional satisfaction, good time, wishes come true, well-being, indulgence, hosting a feast, manifestation, smugness.

Description and meaning:

In this card a happy fat man is sitting with his arms crossed, in the back ground there are nicely place nine cups.

Nine of cups is a wish card. The person will have many friends. This card indicates material pleasure, good luck, stillness and wealth. When this card appears in the reading it shows name, fame and money. The person will make show off of his wealth but will not share it with others.

The nine of cups is a card of satisfaction, wishes coming true, feeling on top of the world. When this card appears, you are feeling good or likely to feel good very soon.

Reverse:

May have lost all wealth. Disappointment, envy, emotional void, ungrateful, self-centered.

Ten of Cups

Key words:

Emotional fulfilment, love to share, ecstasy, happy home, blessed union, idealization, extended family, country living.

Description and meaning:

This card shows a rainbow, happy couple and dancing kids. Rainbow indicates happy situation. It means happy married life. Spending happy time with family. True friendship end of quarrel. Time to come close in a relationship. Happiness in home, worshiping and good omen.

When this card appears, you have enough happiness to share with those around you. Emotional connection and home life are blessed.

Reverse:

Ingratitude, self-pity, separation, divorce, dysfunctional relationship, impossible dreams. No love, no happiness in family. Misunderstanding and end of friendship.

Page of Cups

Key words:

Romantic, naive, sensitive, kind, playful, sweet child, messages from unconscious, listening, ready for love, emotional news.

Description and meaning:

In this card a very beautiful person is holding a cup. There is a fish in the cup and water in the background.

Page means messenger, lucky man, good planner, helpful, nice person. This card indicates beginning of romance. Cup also indicates connection with mind and emotions.

The page of cups is a youthful, sensitive, imaginative person. His heart is open to love and messages from higher self. He is willing to share his deepest feelings and dearest dreams.

This page has a deepest desire to express himself creatively. This card also indicates messages from your dreams and love letters. When this card appears in a reading the person will be a creative artist. It is a time to prepare for a new venture. When this card appears the expression of the person will be like that of opposite gender.

Reverse:

Emotional immaturity, neediness, emotionally dependent, emotional defences, not listening to intuition. Bad habits, unrealistic thoughts, lazy, not trustable.

Knight of Cups

Key words:

Spiritual seeker, performer, idealistic, artist, poetic, charming, seductive, travel by water, wet weather.

Description and meaning:

In this card a well-dressed man looking like a soldier is travelling on white horse. He is holding a cup. There is a flowing river. Horse is not running in speed that means he is emotional. He is going towards his dreams and true love.

The knight of cups is a romantic, artistic, impulsive person. He follows his heart and dreams, shares his vision with others. He loves art and beauty. His mind is like that of person of age 20-40 years. He likes flowers, cards, gifts and romance.

When this card appears in a reading new relationship, travel, newness in life will e experienced.

He can be emotionally unstable, quickly fluctuating from high to low feeling. He can be very loving and passionate, but his feelings can change quickly. He is a dreamer who may not think of long-term result of his actions. He will work in cooperation with others and get his work done. He has good power of imagination.

Reverse:

Overly sensitive, flighty, dysfunctional escapism, false feelings, creative block, hidden feelings. No trust in love, indecisiveness, his emotions will work against him.

Queen of Cups

Key words:

Wisdom, sensitive, receptive, affectionate, virtuous, psychic, counsellor, dreamer, emotional, people pleasure, in love.

Description and meaning:

The queen is sitting on her sinhasan chair, she is holding a cup and looking at her dreams. She is artistic, creative, secretive, beautiful. The jug is closed, so this lady is not able to express her emotions. She is honest and loyal. Caretaker of family and husband, she is responsible. She is living a good life with no scarcity. She can earn money through imagination and art. She loves animals.

The queen of cups is a mature, sensitive, romantic person. She is an empathetic, soothing and kind listener. She helps others to understand their own emotions. She is connected to her higher self. She pays close attention to her feelings and intuition. She is a loving mother.

Reverse:

Ugly and not trustable, Lack of emotional boundaries, taking on other's pain, giving too much emotionally, emotions overwhelm.

King of Cups

Keywords:

Emotional strength, validating, faithful, comforting, old-fashioned, emotional control, compassionate, counsellor, knowing your boundaries.

Description and meaning:

King of cups is very positive. In the middle of the ocean, he is sitting on his sinhasan. He is holding a cup and emperor's tool. Water is flowing and there is a dolphin.

King of cups represents age of 40 yrs or more. He is emotional, trustable, loving, mature. He may be playing a role of uncle, elder brother, grandfather. He is peaceful, understanding and systematic. He may have received lot of love in past. He may be a businessman, artist, good looking. He will be an affectionate elder. He is an achiever in life. He would have seen the world. He is rich and successful.

The king of cups is emotionally mature. He is able to observe his emotions and respond wisely. He is a wonderful counsellor and adviser. He has a big heart, is extremely caring and makes a wonderful husband and father.

He may seem emotionally detached, but this is only because he is calm and mature, not because he doesn't care.

Reverse:

Emotionally hardened, unfeeling, private emotional pain, emotionally unavailable, lost in love, emotionally overbearing, excessively emotional. Aged and irritating nature, complaining nature, attention seeker, not trustable, selfish.

Ace of Pentacles

Key words:

Opportunity, seed, gift, money, new responsibility, available resources, good health.

Description and meaning:

Hand with a pentacle is coming out of cloud. Below there is a flower garden. It indicates a good time. When this card appears once take risk and can move on with money making ideas. Can expect success. One can get bonus, new job, promotion, gifts etc. Money can come any way.

When this card appears in a reading one can get name, fame and promotion. Students can expect good results, may get scholarship, sudden gain, good rewards, gain from ancestor's property. Security and stability, improvement in financial conditions.

This card represents opportunity for real, concrete growth. It can be a beginning of a new project, a chance to improve health. This is the time to strengthen your roots, to ground and centre your body, and to begin to build foundation for the future.

Reverse:

Clinging to material sources, fear of loss, unwise investments, disconnection from physical body, unhealthy behaviour. Loss in gambling, bad results in study, outgoing flow of money, waste of money.

Two of Pentacles

Key words:

Juggling, keeping busy, trading, flexibility, travel for business, organization.

Description and meaning:

The person in this card is dancing with two pentacles. Both pentacles are tied with rope. Two boats in the sea, one is near and other is far.

The two of pentacles represents multitasking and nimble movement. Have to select one out of two options. It is time to work hard. He is manipulative in money matters. This card indicates separation of property or business.

This card indicates you to be flexible and adaptable. Take life's ups and downs as they come, go with the flow.

He may be a banker or a businessman. He may be a money lender. This card could also be telling you to "follow the money". You may have to travel or move house in order to make money.

Reverse:

Lack of productivity, emotions getting in the way of work, ineffective multitasking, missed opportunity, problem with business travel. Quarrel and disputes. Incomplete projects.

Three of Pentacles

Key words:

Assistance, contribution, teamwork, apprenticeship, employment, commitment.

Description and meaning:

When this card appears, a project is beginning to manifest. This person has good nature, can become a successful businessman. It indicates good time to start a new project.

Three of pentacles indicate air, water and fire element. Can achieve success with hard work. People are coming together to make something happen. The foundation is laid for the new house. The intentions you have sent into the universe are beginning to come to fruition. It is time to access your project and see if it is in line with your larger goals. Choose the right activity and partnership to lead you towards your long-term goals.

Reverse:

Uncooperative, poor work, criticism, feeling underappreciated for your work. Lack of focus towards growth opportunities, lack of money, lack of planning.

Four of Pentacles

Key words:

Possession, protectiveness, greed, stagnation, security, worry, saving resources.

Description and meaning:

In this card a person is trying to balance a pentacle in hand. He has placed two pentacles below his feet. In the background you can see a big city.

He is a miser, holds on to money. If this card appears in a reading for husband, he will hold on to things in heart. When this card appears matters of security and control are important.

You have reached a point where you feel secure with your resources, but you don't want to change anything. It is time to save money. Should be careful while making partnership. This person will try for easy money.

You may be protecting your money, your job, your time, your home, your possessions, or your material wealth. You are creating an opportunity to learn, grow and acquire more.

The four of pentacles indicate that you have a firm foundation. At this time sitting firmly is the right thing to do.

Reverse:

Throwing away, over generous, asceticism, greed. Over spending, unexpected expenses. If reading for home, there will be a delay.

Five of Pentacles

Key words:

Poverty, going without, ill health, loss, asceticism, misery.

Description and meaning:

In this card two poor men are passing through below stain glass. Outside there is snow fall. This is very dangerous card. There could be cheating with money. It indicates bankruptcy, betrayal in job or loneliness.

When this card appears your sense of security is threatened. Should be careful about money. There will be separation with spouse, breakup in love affairs. Two people in the card don't have unity, they are seeking help from others.

When this card appears in a reading, you are lacking money or other resources. You may be feeling ashamed or fearful of relying on other's support. Ill health may be preventing you from securing material resources. You may have chosen to forgo some material comfort voluntarily, as a spiritual practice or in support to others.

When this card appears pay attention to the wealth that you have.

Reverse:

Employment, money coming in, victim mentality spending beyond your means, insecure future.

Six of Pentacles

Key words:

Exchange, charity, generosity, loans, gifts, dependence, giving back, gratitude.

Description and meaning:

In this card there is noble, successful, rich businessman. He is giving money to those who are in need. It means loan will be available, work will be done in six months. This is a good card for making money. The person is generous, shares with open heart.

The six of pentacles is about giving and receiving and the balance between them. It could be indicating that you have gratitude for what you have received, by giving to charity or helping others. Pay it back.

Pay attention to how you use your resources and energy. If you are not getting what you expect, look at what you are giving.

In a relationship reading this card is reminding you to pay attention to how you give and take from that person. Balance giving and receiving, if not by money then by other means.

Reverse:

Buried in debt, hoarding wealth, excessive charity, loan denied, exploitation.

Seven of Pentacles

Key words:

Assessment, patience, slow progress, learning from experience, competence.

Description and meaning:

In this card a young guy is tensed. He will succeed after lot of hard work. The seven of pentacles represents a time of pause and assessment. You have been working on some project. Now is the time to stand back and evaluate whether you are on the right path.

With patience one will succeed, do not depend on others. There is lot of money in this card which indicates stability. If things are not working the way you want them to, now is the time to look at what you can change. You are making progress but you have to make some adjustments to achieve mastery.

Try to learn from criticism, you are not failing, you are learning.

Reverse:

Ready to give up, disappointing results, learning from failure, making the same mistakes.

Eight of Pentacles

Key words:

Fine-tuning, perfection, maintenance, hard work, practice, repetition.

Description and meaning:

In this card a person is sitting on the bench and making a trophy. This card means that he is a student who is continuously learning new things. He is passionate about his work. May get new job or promotion.

This card portrays a young man working diligently and happily on a project. He has already completed a great deal of his task and is focused on maintaining the quality of work.

When this card appears in a reading focussed and satisfying work is indicated. It means that soon you will be employed in steady and rewarding work. This is a card of nearing mastery and maintaining effort and focus until the end.

This person is a creative person in fields like jewellery, architecture, carpentry, civil engineer, film maker etc. He is very skilful and has promising future.

Reverse:

Not making visible progress, disappointing pay back, lack of recognition for your hard work, shabby work. No interest to learn new things, lazy, lack of creativity.

Nine of Pentacles

Key words:

Earned rewards, independence, pleasure, luxury, fruits of labour, self-fulfilment.

Description and meaning:

In this card a lady is wearing gown of fruit and flower print. She is holding a bird and standing in a beautiful garden. This card means that there is success after hard work and has lot of fulfilment. She acted with discipline, taming her impulses like she's tamed the bird on her own.

When this card appears, it is time to act with such discipline, you will accomplish more by taming your animal instincts. It indicates material comfort and luxury.

This is a card of prosperity.

Reverse:

Trying to buy self-esteem, unrewarded work, expecting others to take care of you, fear of spending money on yourself.

Ten of Pentacles

Key words:

Permanence, tradition, wealth, legacy, ancestry, family responsibility, security, ancestors.

Description and meaning:

In this card a male and a female are supporting each other. Two curious dogs are seeing people who are standing. Ten of pentacles is a card of physical security.

This card mean that they are very happy family. All generations are happily living together. It could mean a successful financial venture, an inheritance that will provide for all who are concerned. It is an auspicious partnership.

It indicates wedding between family of two business associates. It indicates progress in family business. Unity between all in the family. When this card appears all family members will celebrate social life together. It means success by taking high education.

Reverse:

Issues with settling an estate, selfishness, lacking tradition, attachment to tradition, private tradition, separation in business, fights, conflicts between husband and wife, no peace in spite of having money.

Page of Pentacles

Key words:

Student, practical, careful, steady, collector, messages from nature or body.

Description and meaning:

In this card a young guy is holding a pentacle and thinking about it. In the background there is holy tree and mountains. This means that the person is concerned about money matter since very young age. It represents ambition, beginning of new work, success etc. Even though he is young but he is particular about money. He is an obedient son and will respect all. He is the one on whom all will feel proud. He will be interested in business, share market, manufacturing, jeweller etc.

The page of pentacles is a youthful, dependable, practical person. He is willing to work hard to gain new knowledge and skills. He is often a student; He is a loyal friend who will give useful advice.

This card could also indicate a time to pay attention to your body, the earth and nature. There could be a message in physical world for you.

Reverse:

Short attention-span, unproductive, unfocused, need to apply yourself, overspending, impractical, lack of security, clutter, trouble with paper work.

Knight of Pentacles

Key words:

Dependable, sensual, useful persistence, cautious, stubborn, capable, slow land travel.

Description and meaning:

In this card a strong and safe horse rider is holding a pentacle and looking at the horizon. This card means that he is very practical, honest, disciplined and stable.

The knight of pentacles is a cautious, slow moving, dependable person. He is very careful about everything he does, and sometimes get so caught up in the details that progress is halted. He progresses he makes is sturdy and long-lasting.

He is a good planner, reliable and a good friend. He may sometimes be boring and stubborn, but he gives well thought out and practical advice. He loves comfort and security. He is able to take what he has learned from academic studies, past experiences and use it in a very practical way.

Reverse:

Perfectionism, heavy body, unhealthy behaviour, unhealthy environment, apathy, boredom, mental or physical clutter, disinterest, stuck in a rut.

Queen of Pentacles

Key words:

Nurturer, healer, ecological, protective, hostess, healthy, supportive, practical, principled, calm, a practical friend.

Description and meaning:

In this card a queen is sitting on sinhasana and holding a pentacle on her lap. She is surrounded by nature. It means that he minds is engrossed in money. She is family oriented, understanding, caring and loyal to her family. She teaches discipline and value for money.

She is nature and animal loving. He has acumen to come out of any situation, she respects all, she could be a loyal business woman.

The queen of pentacles is a very practical and organised woman. She is successful in business and creating a secure, comfortable home for herself and those she loves.

By making sensible decisions she has made steady, sustainable progress. She is well grounded and emotionally balanced.

Reverse:

Over indulgence, emotional eating, short term gratification, wastefulness, disconnection with earth, ungrounded, need self care, fearful of change, mismanagement of money or home.

King of Pentacles

Key words:

Loyal business person, pleasure-loving, good with money, conservative, provider, land owner.

Description and meaning:

In this card a king is sitting on an ox headed sinhasana. He is powerful and safe. In the background a prosperous city is seen.

This card mean that the person is enjoying his success and wealth. He is hard working, honest, loyal, clever, creative. He is very close to his family. He may be a head in financial department, C.A., head of company and is financially rich.

The king of pentacles is a successful and ambitious man. He is practical and careful business person. He is a manager or owner of resources. He is a wealthy man, he is careful with his money, but does not mind spending on life luxuries. He is a sensual person who treasures comfort.

A thoughtful, considerate lover, husband and father. He is calm and patient.

Reverse:

Materialism, workaholic, greed, corruption, exploitation, overspending, over eating, jealous, possessiveness.

Ace of Swords

Key words:

New perspective, new plans, will power, sharp mind, making a decision, seeking truth, confidence.

Description and meaning:

In this card a sward is coming out from clouds. On top of the sward there is a crown, decorated with leaves.

When this card appears, you will be presented with an opportunity to use your mind to cut through obstacles. You can turn your dreams into reality with hard work.

There may be a problem to solve which will lead to personal growth. You will have mental focus to make new plans, develop new strategies, and commit to effective action. This card indicates change in perception for old issue. When this card appears, it may be an opportunity to cut away what is unnecessary and leave it behind.

Reverse:

Truth not available, misunderstanding, missing information, deception, cloudy thinking, confusion, giving up.

Two of Swords

Key words:

Impartial, indecision, closed off, conflicting ideas.

Description and meaning:

In this card a blindfolded lady is sitting on a table at the sea. There is a reverse moon in background. She is holding 2 swords in cross position. This means that the person is stuck in a situation.

When the two of swords appear, you are putting off making a decision for now. You may be feeling uncertainty. You may not want to offend or hurt someone involved. The two of swords represent the need for withdrawal. This card indicates that you need to know more facts before making a decision.

The two of swords could also be indicating that you are ignoring your emotions, using logic to deny how you are feeling. You may be denying the truth.

You may be in a state of denial and not accepting mistakes.

Reverse:

Faulty logic, silent treatment, muted truth.

Three of Swords

Key words:

Loss, heartache, sorrow, separation, a necessary sacrifice.

Description and meaning:

In this card three swards are pearsed through a heart. In the background there are rainy clouds. This indicates painful ending of a relationship.

The three of swards indicates some sort of difficult loss. Whether it is loss of relationship, the loss of trust due to betrayal, rejection, losing job, accident, surgery etc.

The loss will not be easy. When you feel pain and do something to fix it, you grow.

Reverse:

Making space for new things, risk of relapse, private sacrifice, meaning less sacrifice, difficulty giving up a habit.

Four of Swords

Key words:

Sleep, respite, mental restoration, self-reflection, "sleep on it".

Description and meaning:

In this card a soldier is sleeping on a grave. There are three swords hanging on the wall. When this card appears in a reading it is time for a break. There could be a situation of fight, it suggests taking decision with peace. Whether you are having a hard time working through the problem. You are starting to feel ill or need some fresh ideas. When four of swords appear in a reading it is time to retreat at the quite place.

The four of swords may be advising you to seek counsel, go to an expert for advice.

Reverse:

Mental overload, much needed break, delayed rest, chaotic environment, integration after a retreat, prolonged vacation.

Five of Swords

Key words:

Disagreement, miscommunication, scattered mind, self-centred, divisive action.

Description and meaning:

In this card a person is holding 3 swords and running away from battle field. It indicates that you may encounter fight or cheating with someone. There could be jealousy and unpleasant environment.

When this card appears in a reading it is time to ask yourself if what you are fighting for is worth it. You may say words which you can never take back. In the process you will be hurting someone. You may try to win just for the sake of winning. This card indicates that you may be repeating patterns that are dysfunctional.

Reverse:

Resolutions, apologies, assessing the damage, debriefing, meditation.

Six of Swords

Key words:

Taking space, space to heal, retreat, transition, gaining perspective, travel over water.

Description and meaning:

In this card they are crossing the river, six swords are placed vertical. When this card appears you are moving away, or planning to move away from pain or confusion. It could also mean that tough time is over, can wait for better time.

This could also mean that you are physically moving away from something destructive such as ending an abusive relationship or moving away from friends who enable abusive behaviour. You may be going away on trip especially over water to gain a new perspective on a difficult situation.

The six of swards also mean that you are gaining distance from the situation to get a wider perspective. This is a time for transition and change is often difficult.

Reverse:

Stuck in an unpleasant situation, or where to turn, afraid to change, need to make changes to heal, irrational clinging, travel delay, money problem, no desired results.

Seven of Swords

Key words:

Strategy, mental tests, deception, gathering information, breaking agreements, fibbing.

Description and meaning:

In this card a person is going holding five swards even before the war has begun, two swards are lying on the ground. This card indicates that the person is a thief, not trustworthy. One should beware of such person. This card indicates that someone can cheat you.

This card is about doing what serves your ends, even if the means are deceptive or manipulative. When this card appears it literally means that you have stolen something from another or someone has stolen from you.

Using clever mind tricks to get what you want is indicated by the seven of swords. This card could indicate guilt over something we have done.

Reverse:

Facing the consequences, being caught, coming clean, guilt, regret, choosing to do the right thing. Beware of betrayal; take right ad vice from wise man.

Eight of Swords

Keywords:

Helpless thoughts, limited options, restricting beliefs, excuses, victim mentality.

Description and meaning:

In this card a lady who is blind folded and wrapped with rope all over the body is seen stuck in between field of swards.

The eight of swards is a card of feeling trapped or limited. This card indicates that you are probably thinking that you have no viable options available. You feel that you lack courage and strength. You may feel weakened by circumstances of your life.

This is a testing time of your patience. People near to you will give you pain. You feel that no one is there to support you. You are imprisoned by your own thinking. You can use your thoughts to remain trapped or you can use them to cut through limitations.

Reverse:

New self awareness, changing your thoughts to change your life, new confidence.

Nine of Swords

Key words:

Mental torment, insomnia, illness, hopelessness, depression, darkest before the dawn.

Description and meaning:

In this card a lady lady is sitting on a bed that has zodiac signs. On the wall adjacent to her there are nine hanging swards.

When this card appears in a reading it means that you are experiencing sleepless nights, worry, anxiety and fear. You will be feeling ill and worried about your health. Worrying is pointless unless it drives us to do something about the troublesome situation.

This card advises us to start confronting our worries and fears. Start taking steps to solve your problems. Talk to someone about what's on your mind.

You are near to your mental ordeal, if you start facing it.

Reverse:

Dysfunctional worry, inner doubt, ignoring anxious feelings, facing your fear. Its time to come out of troubles.

Ten of Swords

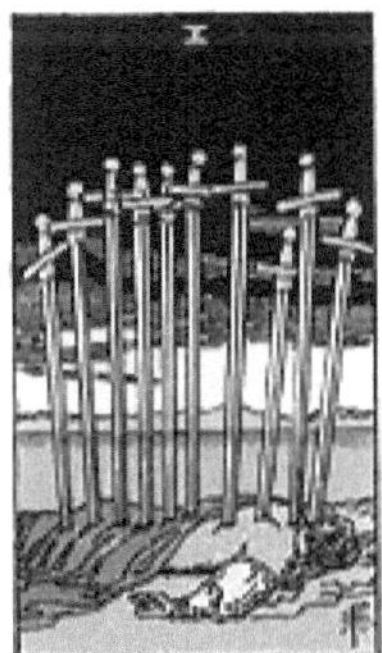

Key words:

Rock bottom, nowhere to go but up, admitting failure, giving up, self pity, quitting.

Description and meaning:

In this card a person is lying dead, he is pierced by ten swards. When the ten of swards appears in a reading it is likely that the situation has become as bad as it possibly can. This is rock bottom, enough is enough, there is nowhere to go but up.

This card indicates death of relationship, complications in illness, back stabbing. Take the lesions you have learned with you so you don't make same mistakes again.

Reverse:

Fresh start, enough is enough, making changes, self doubt, relapse, relief, restoring.

Page of Swords

Keywords:

Curious, idealistic, on guard, learning new skills, alert focused, daring, by the rules.

Description and meaning:

In this card a teenage boy is standing holding the sward. The page of swards is a youthful, cautious, thoughtful person. He seeks truth and justice above all else. He is willing to take risk with communication in order to get closer the truth of the situation. He is a student of communication and can learn a lot about himself through his writing and conversations.

This card could also represent some news that will alert you to the truth.

Reverse:

Misunderstanding, muddled words, can't say what you mean, missed messages, self doubt, lies, speaking without thinking, gossip, betraying secrets.

Knight of Swords

Keywords:

Revolutionary, critical thinking, impatient, truth seeker, know-it-all, self righteous, acting efficiently, fast travel, stormy weather.

Description and meaning:

In this card a person is ridding the horse and going to the battle field, he is holding a sward.

The knight of swards is a sharp minded, direct and idealistic person, He is a great problem solver and debater. He is rational and doesn't let his feeling drive him. He can be head strong and impatient. His communication is very direct and often piercing.

He feels very passionately about his own ideas and will spare no one's feeling in getting his point across. Though he is very intelligent he often jumps to conclusions.

Reverse:

Slow down, think before you speak, choosing to remain silent, regret over words spoken, getting caught up in arguments, defending the wrong things, hurtful words.

Queen of Swords

Keywords:

Self aware, intelligent, honest, fair, self-reliant, reserved wise, protector of truth, self-disciplined, perfectionist, judgemental, analytical, widowed or divorced.

Description and meaning:

In this card a queen is holding a sword and sitting on her sinhaasan. She is raising her hand to do justice.

The queen of swords is a very independent woman. She observes strict rules and regulations. She has great clarity of thoughts and pursues her desires with strength and maturity. She has a very sharp mind and keen sense of justice and fairness.

She may have experienced great loss or sorrow in her life. This experience has enhanced her wisdom. In a reading she may represent that professional counsel should be sought.

Reverse:

Fooling yourself, lacking insight, ignoring feelings, denial, mean words, harsh criticism, gossip, bullying with words.

King of Swords

Keywords:

Judge, intentional, efficient, intelligent, logical, decisive, fair, critical, legal matters, rules and limitations.

Description and meaning:

In this card a king is ruling, he is holding a sword, the atmosphere is soothing. The king of swords is a master mind. He is calm, mature, analytical and intelligent. He uses this quality for justice and truth. His decisions are based on careful thoughts.

He is committed to his own truth. He will not bend to peer pressure or social norms. He is assertive and can also be aggressive in pursuit of justice.

Reverse:

Check your facts, examine your motivations, bending the truth, muddled thoughts, punishment, doesn't fit the crime, cruel words, using position of leadership to hurt others, slander, not trustable.

Ace of Wands

Keywords:

Yes, idea, passion, inspiration, birth, opportunity, advancement, light-hearted.

Description and meaning:

In this card through the clouds a wand is appearing in the hand. It indicates success after hardship. When this card appears look for a new opportunity, new beginning, newness in life, support of god. It also indicates power of winning. Wand is majestic.

This is a new bright idea, a burst of creative energy. A source of inspiration, excitement, enthusiasm and energy for something new is available. Now is your chance to be courageous.

This card can also indicate new life conception or birth. In a love reading if Ace of wands appears it means passion, excitement and fun. In a career reading when this card appears look for opportunities to be creative and express enthusiasm.

Reverse:

Fatigue, uninspired, overburdened, hyperactivity, private projects. New beginning is not started. Know the past before making new beginning,

Two of Wands

Keywords:

Choice, potential, contemplation, threshold, planning.

Description and meaning:

In this card a person is holding a wand and a globe. He is looking at the tides in the sea. On his backside there is a fort and flowers on the sides. This is a business card.

When this card appears in a reading you are at a point where you have the power to choose. You are fitted with creative force. It can indicate a waiting period. It is a time to look back at where you have come from and forward to where you want to go. You are not stuck with only one option. Be brave, be bold, be true to yourself. You have power within you to create your own destiny. Success through passion and vision.

Reverse:

Stuck, unprepared, bad intentions, no options, rushed, unrealistic. Loss of freedom, doubts in partnership, loss of opportunity.

Three of Wands

Keywords:

Setting out, authority, boldness, initiative, supervising, long-term plans, travel, trade.

Description and meaning:

In this card a person is holding one of the three wand and looking at tides in the sea. When this card appears, it indicates that you have set things in motion and there is no turning back now.

You know what you want to do and you have the confidence to do it. It also indicates business of import or export. The two wands indicate additional support. With bright future ahead of you, it is an ideal time to let go of past hurts.

This card may indicate foreign travel. The three of wands suggests equality and cooperation. When this card appears, growth is certain.

Reverse:

Apprehension, travel delays, delayed projects, need for more planning, unprepared, under educated, afraid to commit.

Four of Wands

Keywords:

Home coming, arrival, harvest, ceremony, achievement, property, firm foundation, gratitude, happy home.

Description and meaning:

In this card a well decorated four wands are placed. Two persons are holding flower bouquet. When this card appears in a reading it's time to celebrate your accomplishments. It shows happy family. This is a card that indicates progress. You have had success in your journey. Take time to honour your hard work.

The four of wands indicates successful completion of work. It could be a birthday, a wedding, an anniversary, new home, picnic, holiday, achievement, establishment, good luck.

This card indicates a need to mark a new life transition with ceremony or ritual. Celebrate yourself.

Reverse:

Stressful preparations, ingratitude, troublesome family gathering, private celebration, unsupportive environment. Chances of making wrong decisions.

Five of Wands

Keywords:

Competition, contest, games, problem solving, struggle, brainstorming, hassles.

Description and meaning:

In this card five men are fighting with each other or playing a competition or game. When this card appears expect conflict of some kind. The life of a person is like a warrior. You have to fight every battle with courage, ultimately you will win.

It could possibly be negative, such as petty hassles, arguments, and clashing of personalities. It also represents friendly competition such as in games or contest.

This card could indicate petty hassles and annoyances. Don't make more of your problems than they actually are.

Reverse:

Apologies, admitting a mistake, avoiding conflicts, backing down, inner conflict.

Six of Wands

Keywords:

Leadership, support, success, advancement, winning, recognition, public opinion.

Description and meaning:

In this card a confident man like a leader is riding the horse. He is holding a long wand which is having a flower garland. There are similar five more wands.

When this card appears, you should take pride in your ability to lead and inspire others. This card also indicates success, promotion, fulfilment, helping friends, name, fame, money, awards.

You have works hard and receiving recognition for your accomplishments. Others are looking at you for guidance.

Reverse:

Difficulty in leadership, betrayal, lack of teamwork, egoism, difficulty with recognition, stressful celebration, corruption, lack of confidence.

Seven of Wands

Keywords:

Steadfastness, tenacity, courage, persistence, defending views, facing opposition.

Description and meaning:

In this card a person is trying to defend himself using the wand. Other wands in the picture looks like attacking on him.

When this card appears in a reading be prepared to take a stand for what you believe in.

There are big forces at work against you. By facing up this challenge you will refine your principles, gain courage, develop your character, can be ready to achieve mastery.

When this card appears ask yourself what you truly believe. If you are confident in your perspective then don't back down.

Reverse:

Backing down, unable to speak up, stubborn resistance, battling inner doubts.

Eight of Wands

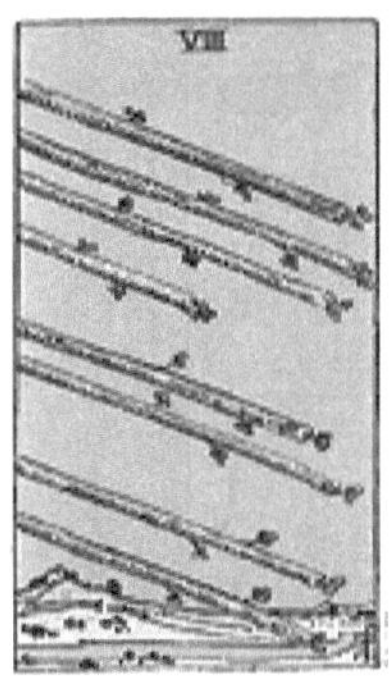

Keywords:

Advancement, swiftness, speed, rapid communication, streamlining, flow.

Description and meaning:

In this card eight wands are moving towards village for fighting. When this card appears, things are happening or about to happen quickly. This is the card of things set in motion, rapid communication and intense energy. Matter at hand will quickly be resolved often in satisfactory ways.

A warning here may be to ask yourself what you are rushing into and why? If this rapid action is in line with your ultimate goal then enjoy the ride.

This card may appear when romance is passionate. Love at first sight. Expect a message that you have been waiting for. Travel by air is indicated by the eight of wands.

Reverse:

Impatience, delays, restlessness, miscommunication, wrong turns, overlooking details, risky behaviour, sudden breakthrough, making it to the next level.

Nine of Wands

Keywords:

Defensiveness, caution, protection, accumulation, strong character, old habits, suspicion.

Description and meaning:

In this card a sad person is standing while holding a wand. At the back of him there are eight wands which indicate he is ready to fight the battle. He has wound on his head and is bleeding.

This card indicates that he has gone through tough times. He has been working hard all life time. He is in double mind. The nine of wands is a card about wisdom and strength gained through experience. When this card appears in a reading think back to a time when you have been in a similar situation. What lessons did you learn then that you can apply now?

This card could be serving as a warning. Sometimes when we expect the worst, that's exactly what we end up getting. If you are not satisfied with your current situation, you can make a choice to change that too. Keep patience, be ready to do something new in order to change situation.

Reverse:

Defensiveness, weariness, assumptions, inexperienced, subjective advice.

Ten of Wands

Keywords:

Success, work, responsibility, overburdened, weight, burnout, trapped, pride.

Description and meaning:

In this card a man is carrying heavy wands and moving towards village. It means that he is burdened. You will succeed but at the same time you will have to bear the burden.

When this card shows up there is lot of responsibility, you feel overburdened or resentful. Don't think your work as a burden, take it easy and finish it off. When we try to do too much, we are often unable to do anything effectively. We miss new inspiration and growth. We may also be at risk of physical and emotional injury.

Delegate responsibility to someone else.

Reverse:

Overwhelmed, procrastination, busy work, unproductive, wasting time, relief, delegation of responsibility, fresh start, new perspective.

Page of Wands

Keywords:

Free spirit, news, curious, enthusiastic, willing, seeker, ambitious, fearless, candid, newness, energetic, outgoing.

Description and meaning:

In this card a young man is holding a vertical wand and looking at sky with hope. He is innovative and creative. He is keen for music, art, acting. He is enthusiastic and hardworking, so he makes his own position.

He is excited and willing to embark upon new adventures. He is healthy and full of vital energy. He is learning to use his energy to meet his goals.

This card could indicate new beginning or a new project. This card could also indicate exciting news.

Reverse:

Blocked inspiration, overly serious, overwhelmed with ideas, secret projects, flightiness.

Knight of Wands

Keywords:

Forward-thinking, adventures, spontaneous, temperamental, exciting, passionate, flamboyant, hasty, rebellious, competitive, motivating, taking action, moving, land travel, heat.

Description and meaning:

In this card a person is riding the horse in speed and is moving to fight. He is holding a wand. He seems to be from a king's family.

The knight of wands is an energetic, charismatic, confident person. He likes adventure and is a flirt by nature. He seeks self growth and always looking for challenge. He can be competitive and dynamic. He has desire and ability to grow.

Reverse:

Lack of inspiration, no energy, fear of failure, reckless, thoughtless, acting out.

Queen of Wands

Keywords:

Creative, independent, self-confident, passionate, romantic, leader, bold, outgoing, energetic, influential, dramatic, determination, friendly, optimistic.

Description and meaning:

In this card a queen is sitting on sinhasan. She is holding a sunflower in one hand and a wand in another hand. There is a black cat near her feet.

The queen of wands is mature, confident, passionate person. She is dedicated to her pursuits in career, family and love. She is popular and fun. People love to be around her; she is generous and love to make others smile.

She is super sexy. She does what she loves, takes chances in following her passion. She sometimes uses her charisma and sex appeal to manipulate others. She can also be impulsive and has quick temper.

Reverse:

Misuse of power, catty, excluding, mean, projecting negative feelings, bullying, irritable, blocked sexuality, frigidity.

King of Wands

Keywords:

Courageous, generous, authentic, leader, powerful, risk-taker, creative, dominating, confident, self-reliant, motivating, proud, self-expressive.

Description and meaning:

In this card a king is sitting on sinhasana, he is holding a wand. There is a lizard near his feet. He is looking towards west.

The king of wands is a natural leader. He is devoted to his family and those he leads. He is charming, kind and is motivated to take positive actions. He is decisive and courageous and takes risks based on his gut feelings.

He likes excitement, competition and challenges. He is not rigid in his thinking and is receptive to different point of view. He acts and speaks with integrity. He is a person in high position in organisations or in social circle.

Reverse:

Unauthentic, selfish, egoistic, risky behaviour, not trustable, narrow minded, always worrying.

Chapter 6

Yes & No Reading.

This reading technique with Tarot Cards is very easy and accurate for finding answers in yes or no.

1) Be ready with the specific question in your mind.

2) Pray to Tarot Cards & Tarot Family to give you the answer is yes or no.

3) Start drawing card one by one from the count from 1 to 13.

4) If any card of Ace appears in the first 13 cards the answer is yes 100%.

5) If any card of Ace appears in card number 14 to 26 the answer is 75% yes.

6) If any card of Ace appears in card number 27 to 39 the answer is 50% yes.

7) If no card of Ace appears in first 26 cards, the answer is no.

Chapter 7

Past Present & Future Reading.

This reading technique with Tarot Cards is very easy and accurate for finding answers in yes or no.

1) Be ready with the specific question in your mind.

2) Pray to Tarot Cards & Tarot Family to give you the past, present and future reading.

3) Start drawing three cards.

4) The 1st card will represent reading for the past. The 2nd card will represent reading for the present and the 3rd card will represent the reading for the future.

Chapter 8

Daily Reading.

This reading technique with Tarot Cards will give you predictions and guidance about daily events.

1) Pray to Tarot Cards & Tarot Family to give you the daily reading.

2) Start drawing three cards for the day.

3) The three cards are based on hourly based. The 1st card is about morning 6 am to 12 pm. The 2nd card is about afternoon 12 pm to 6 pm. And the 3rd card is about night 6 pm to 12 am.

4) Each card will show to events and situations through the day.

Chapter 9

Monthly Reading.

This reading technique with Tarot Cards will give you predictions and guidance about monthly events.

1) Pray to Tarot Cards & Tarot Family to give you the monthly reading.

2) Start drawing two cards for the month.

3) Take one extra card. The 3rd card will show you the important situation.

4) The two cards of the month represent 1st fifteen days and 2nd 15 days of the month.

Chapter 10

Yearly Reading.

This reading technique with Tarot Cards will give you predictions and guidance about yearly events.

1) Pray to Tarot Cards & Tarot Family to give you the yearly reading.

2) Start drawing two cards for each month from Jan to Dec. Two cards for each month to be placed one after another.

3) Take one extra card. The 13th card will show you the important situation.

4) If two major arcana cards appear together it will be very important month.

5) The two cards per month represents 1st fifteen days and 2nd 15 days of the month.

Chapter 11

Relationship Reading.

This reading technique with Tarot Cards will help you to understand your relationship.

1) Be ready with the specific relationship reading.

2) Pray to Tarot Cards & Tarot Family to give you the reading about the relationship.

3) Start drawing card one by one from the count 1 to 7.

4) Place the cards from 1 to 7 as per the diagram given below.

5) Each card will give you the reading as mentioned in the chart below.

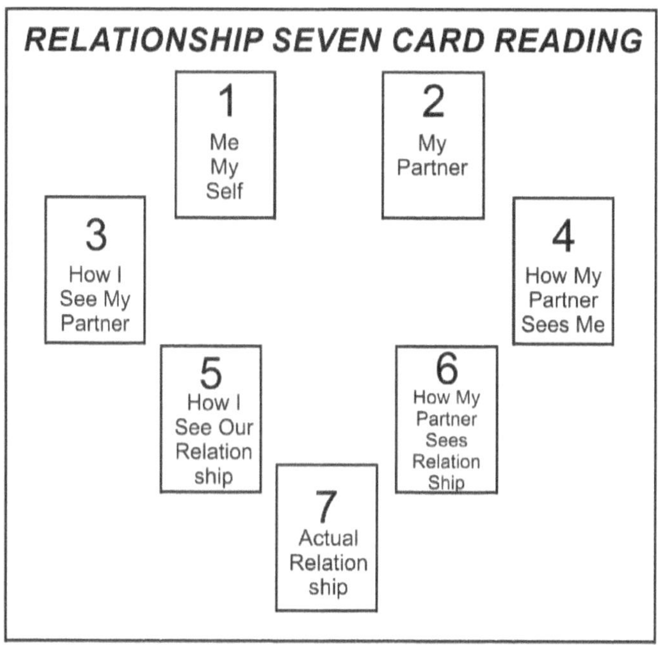

RELATIONSHIP SEVEN CARD READING
1
Me
My
Self
2
My
Partner
3
How I
See My
Partner
4
How My
Partner
Sees Me
5
How I
See Our
Relation
ship
6
How My
Partner
Sees
Relation
Ship
7
Actual
Relation
ship

Chapter 12

Mind, Body & Soul Reading.

This reading technique with Tarot Cards enables the reading of mind, body and soul. With this reading you can find out what is happening in the mind, body and soul of a person.

1) Have a clear intent in your mind about doing the reading of a specific person.

2) Pray to Tarot Cards & Tarot Family to give you the reading.

3) Shuffle the card deck. Start drawing three cards.

4) Place the card in left, centre and right.

5) The left card is about the mind. The centre card is about the mind and the right card is about the soul.

6) Each card will exactly show you the accurate reading about person.

7) With this card reading you can also do the counselling of the person for whom you are doing the reading. And you can exactly read the person and take your decisions as per your reading.

Chapter 13

How to do the reading with Tarot Cards?

Tarot cards are a family of 78 cards. They are live energy and consciousness. They give us answers through their mystical powers.

Whenever you do the reading with Tarot Cards first energize the cards. Then pray to Tarot family to help you in the reading process.

Seek permission from Tarot family to enable you with the reading for specific person who comes to you for reading purpose.

With full respect and faith begin your reading. Tarot family always guides you and protects you during the reading session.

Also invoke arch angle Raphael and Michael before starting the reading. Tap with your index finger on the Tarot Desk at the time of starting the reading.

Always remember that you are a channel through which the Tarot family gives the answers. Never fall into ego trap that you are doing the reading. You are just a medium.

Don't initiate the reading with negative mindset. Always practice reading with positive and happy state of mind.

Chapter 13

How to cut the energy after the Reading.

After the reading session is complete, disconnect the energy of the person from the cards.

Hold the Tarot deck in to your palm of both hands and command three times cut cut cut.

Let the energy and thoughts of the person for whom the reading is done be now get disconnected now.

Offer gratitude to the Tarot family through the bottom of your heart. Thank the cards for assisting you in the reading.

Next time whenever you wish to do the reading, Tarot family will be too happy to help you.

Thank you. Thank you. Thank you.